About

How do you go from training lc
how do you do it well? The boι
presenters to be successful wι
comfortably to making audienι

There are ideas and tips for preparation and suggestions of
information to find out before you go. Seasoned professionals offer
ideas and suggestions to help you be successful as you deal with,
and present to, new cultures and countries.

Praise

The book is chock-filled with practical tips to prepare you
physically and emotionally before, during, and after your trip. By
sharing stories of the challenges she has personally confronted
and overcome, Renie McClay opens up the world to the reader,
making an emotional connection that sparks deep learning. The
inclusion of Geert Hofstede's cultural dimensions model provides a
sound theoretical grounding without bogging things down in
academic nomenclature. I wholeheartedly recommend this no-frills,
no-fluff book to anyone involved in global training and presenting.
-Vincent L. Cyboran, *Ed.D., Associate Professor, Chair, Graduate
Program in Training and Development, Roosevelt University*

There are a number of books on how to conduct business in a
global economy, but Renie McClay fills a critical gap for those of
us in Learning and Performance. *111 Ideas to Engage Global
Audiences* is a great introduction for anyone who is considering
training outside the US and one I wish had been available when I
was starting my Global training career.
-Sandy Stricker, *Director, Sales Learning, ADP*

Renie McClay has written a valuable primer for the uninitiated and
an excellent volume of reminders for anyone who travels abroad
on business. As a first time expat, I relived my entire first 18
months' experience in these pages, nodding with recognition and
agreement as I read along.
-Charles Gremillion, *Senior Director Full Service Brand
Management, Asia Pacific, Hilton Worldwide*

111 Ideas to Engage Global Audiences

Author: Renie McClay, MA, CPLP

Cover Design: Helder Magalhaes

Learniappe Publishing
info@learniappe.com

ISBN-13: 978-1482610536
ISBN-10: 1482610531

PRINTED IN THE UNITED STATES OF AMERICA
First Edition

Introduction

How does a global passion begin?

Personally, I had some life-expanding events that lead me that direction. It started when I attended my first sales training class when I was 22, and instantly knew that was the career I wanted. And when I got my first training job, I knew that having a rewarding job I enjoyed was an incredible adventure and I never wanted to leave that career path.

I was born and raised in Kansas and Missouri, in the heart of the American Midwest. As a result, I did not experience a lot of cultural diversity. At the age of 25, I took a trip to Europe, where I drove with a friend on a road trip from Germany to Austria, Italy, Switzerland, France, and the Netherlands that blew my horizons wide-open. *Bam*, I was hooked. I did not know their language, which added to the excitement and adventure of experiencing such different cultures. I would find myself walking around in a restaurant and pointing to what I wanted to order. Friendly people helped when we found ourselves lost on a mountaintop in Italy—talking and gesturing, they drew a map in the dirt with a stick to show us how to get back. It was so amazing and life changing—I was hooked on global travel and knew I wanted to figure out how to incorporate that into my work.

The next stage of my life was as a parent. I had the chance to bring my son with me to Ghana and India to do humanitarian work. If the initial Europe trip was life-expanding, these trips were positively life-altering. Helping people, getting to know them, seeing how they live—it fueled and continued the global passion. I hope this book helps to fuel your global passion, too.

Renie McClay

Contents

Getting Started

How do you go from training locally to training globally? And then how do you do it well? This book offers at least 111 ideas on the topic.

There are many things that are different when interacting with global or multi-cultural audiences. Some of the key areas are:

- Environment
- Time
- Communication
- Technology
- Culture
- Language

We will explore these topics and more. This book is designed to give you some valuable questions to ask and some ideas to help you to be successful as you train global or cross-cultural audiences. There will still be a lot you learn on your own, but this book can help get you started.

Some questions to ask before training a global audience for the first time:

- What do I need to know about the culture?
- What do I need to know about language skills?
- What is their native language?
- Will we train in their native language?
- In what language should I create my materials? Will translation be helpful?
- If the training is done in English, do they understand English? Do they speak and read English? To what degree – how would you describe their level of proficiency?

A Little Something Extra

If participants are being trained in a language other than their native language, create materials rich with content. It will give the group a chance to read AND hear the content, improving their understanding. If possible, send them the materials in advance so they can become familiar with unfamiliar terms and start the learning process.

Always plan for unexpected events, such as weather and/or power failures or surges. Finding what you need is not as easy as making a trip to a local Office Depot to get what you need.

Know Before You Go

Planning a trip abroad, especially business trip, can be a very difficult undertaking. There are many things you can do to make sure your trip goes smoothly. The key thing to know is to plan in advance. Having a checklist of things to do helps you remember what has been done and what needs to be done. In this chapter, we will talk about the steps you can take before you go on a trip so that you will not have to worry when you get there.

Trip Planning

- Allow for a recovery day on the front and back end of the trip. It allows for time zone adjusting and (hopefully) getting some sleep after a long flight. You will be glad you did.
- Check early about passports and visa requirements, as countries vary. Some countries require that your passport have an expiration

date at least six months after the end of the trip, and some countries require a visa for entering. To save yourself stress, start early.

- Check to see if shots or medications are recommended for travel to the area you are visiting.

- When traveling with medications, use the original, marked container. If it is a controlled substance, check to see if you need to bring a copy of the prescription.

- Check the Transportation Security Administration (TSA) website for the most current regulations: www.tsa.gov. Also check airline allowances for luggage.

- You may find it helpful to bring enough local currency to pay for the hotel and maybe a couple of meals. Local banks will most likely have the best exchange rate.

- Plan your airport and hotel transportation prior to leaving home. Trust me—one less detail to worry about when arriving is good. Use official transportation and not a person with a sales pitch as you are leaving the airport.

- Have the address and phone number of your hotel printed out and keep it with you, including in the local language (for example, Chinese).
- Verify that packages shipped ahead arrived at the correct location, in case you need to bring along back up.

My very first trip to Canada, I got to customs in Toronto and they asked me my purpose for being there. I, of course, answered honestly and told them "to train a class." Without another word, I was whisked off to immigration, questioned for an hour, and was finally told I had to buy a $300 work permit or go home. I bought the work permit, but could have avoided a lot of wasted time had I just done my homework and known in advance what I needed.

~ Sandy Stricker

Ask a local contact what to expect regarding:

- *Timeliness*: You, as a trainer, need to be on time. However, some countries are event-focused, not time-focused. Ask when to expect your audience to arrive, take breaks, serve meals, and close the session.

- *Smoking and Cell Phone Etiquette*: They vary around the world. Make sure you find out the proper etiquette from your local contact.

- *Attire*: Before you go, do some research or ask your contact person about appropriate attire for your meeting/training.

- *Classroom Sensitivities*: Depending on different countries and cultures, your audience may react to your gender and/or your classroom management style. It is always good to find out in advance about gender sensitivities and/or management considerations. Also, countries vary as far as alcohol consumption at lunch.

- *Logistics*: Sending your material in advance can make your job a lot easier, so it is important for you to get the proper shipping address of the location where you can send your material. If you cannot ship your material in advance, send it electronically, and make arrangements to have it ready. Know the paper size.

- *Power/Voltage:* Communicate with your contact person about your technology, audio/visual, and power needs. Bring appropriate adapters. Ask if there is anything you should know regarding storms, power outages or surges.

I have been told in both Africa and India that if it rains, people may not come. It isn't that they don't want to come; it is because they likely cannot get there. They may be coming in from villages without paved roads. During a strong rainstorm in Kumasi, Ghana, I witnessed the streets become rivers. Drivers stopped on both sides of the "road" and waited for the water level to lower enough to not stall out the vehicles. Weather can be a determining factor anywhere—a snowstorm can close airports and prevent participants from attending. But common circumstances can look pretty different based on where you are.

Location

- Learning about a country's history can help you connect with your audience, as well as give you a sense of culture and traditions.
- Knowing country's/city's geography can help you learn to navigate in a new place. It can also provide some interesting conversation fodder.
- Learning about what is going on in current events and arts in that country can give you something to talk about with your audience.

Culture and Customs

- When choosing your attire for your presentation, know that some cultures are sensitive to certain colors. Make sure you find out before you go, so you can plan accordingly.

> *I facilitate CPLP certification preparation workshops in a lot of Islamic countries to Muslim audiences in the Middle East and Southeast Asia. In respect to my participants and local customs, I am careful about how I dress. I make sure I cover my shoulders and knees, and I watch my neckline. In some cases, I wear an abaya. In all cases, I bring a pashmina for extra coverage, should the need arise. I also pack a long skirt. Being an outgoing and expressive person, I pay attention to my body language and resist the habit of shaking hands (unless I'm offered a hand first) and the urge to touch people—on the arm, on the hand, on the shoulder—anywhere. What I have learned is to not be overly sensitive or scared, and to apologize—immediately—when I make a mistake. I have found people of all cultures to be patient & forgiving.*
> *~ Trish Uhl*

- Learn a few greetings and some key words in your audience's native language. It will help strengthen relationships and build rapport.

- Learning about gestures and bowing or shaking hands can also be helpful. Depending on the country and culture, make sure you know their preferences.

- Learning about religions and holidays that people follow in particular countries can help you plan your schedule and training.

> *Adaptability is an important quality for all trainers. When you add the global element, it becomes essential for success.*
> *~Terrence Donahue*

A Little Something Extra

Be prepared to plan an agenda, some exercises, and your interaction with the group. Don't plan on taking your U.S. curriculum around the world successfully with no thought or modifications. Each audience will have preferences and how they are accustomed to learning, therefore it is important to be prepared for a variety of responses and adapt accordingly. Make role plays, simulations, case studies, and exercises meaningful to the audiences. Use local sports, music references, or local geography—things they can relate to.

> *When planning a six-week curriculum for India, I worked with a local contact. When I told him that I wanted tables brought in for the training, he insisted that the participants could stack materials on their laps, that "they were used to that." We were spending quite a bit of money on this training, so I was politely insistent that people would learn more if they were physically comfortable and had easy access to materials.*
> ~ *Vince Cyboran*

Audience Analysis

It is very important to analyze your audience before you arrive at your training site. It not only helps you to identify your audience, but also it helps you to understand them, as well. By answering these questions, you will better prepare for your presentation.

- Who are the people that will be attending? How many participants?
- What are their jobs, levels of education, interests, and skill level?
- Where do they come from: the city, the country?

- What is going on in their country right now regarding politics, holidays, transportation, work issues, economy, leaders, and the weather?
- What will their attitude be coming to your program? Will they be vacationers, explorers, prisoners? What resistance should you anticipate? Any suggestions on how to address the resistance?
- What problem or challenge will the workshop address?
- Have they been selected to come, forced to come, or offered the opportunity?
- What do they already know about your topic?
- What do they need and want to know about your topic?
- What does their management want them to be able to do as a result of their participation in your program?
- What are their classroom/learning preferences?
- What are their technology skills, if appropriate?
- Who has the best language skills (if helpful)?
- What will the manager's role be? Will they be in the room? What about follow up?

A Little Something Extra

Here are some resources that may be helpful to you before you travel and as part of your preparation for training in a new country:

Websites

CNN News and CNN World News

American Chamber of Commerce for specific countries (for example, www.amcham.org.hk)

Country websites (for example, www.Australia.gov.au)

Wikipedia

Publications

Harvard Business Review (@HarvardBiz on Twitter)

Gestures: The Dos and Taboos of Body Language,
    Roger Axtell

Kiss, Bow, or Shake Hands, Terri Morrison, Wayne A. Conaway (there are now continent specific versions available)

The World is Flat, Thomas L. Friedman

Training for Multiple Cultures, ASTD Infoline, Andrea Edmundson

When Cultures Collide: Leading Across Cultures, Richard D. Lewis

There are more than 111 ideas presented in this book. Some will be relevant to your situation and some will not. There are many lessons learned through experience when traveling and working in a new environment. The goal is for these ideas to help minimize challenges and increase success.

Traveling

Depending on your destination, going abroad will involve some travel time. With proper planning and preparation, you can make that time manageable and pleasant. In this chapter, we will talk about how you can utilize some tips to help minimize discomfort and make your travel comfortable.

Tips for Overcoming Jetlag

- Work hard to stay hydrated. Avoid diuretics while traveling—-namely, caffeine and alcohol. They get in the way of staying hydrated and will increase jet lag symptoms. (Don't be mad at me; it is advice from the Center for Disease Control.)
- Whenever possible, sleep on the plane if it is nighttime at your destination.
- If possible, start to adjust your sleep schedule to the new time zone before you leave. Even an hour or two will help.

Trish takes frequent long-haul flights. She has some self care tips to share:

Staying hydrated means your skin, too! Pack facial moisturizer and hand lotion as well. My favorites are Rx Systems maximum strength moisturizer and Crabtree & Evelyn ultra-moisturizing hand therapy. Make sure you moisturize before, during and after the flight. For example, on a long-haul flight, I moisturize my skin 3-4 times in-flight—in addition to the original application.

Not just for First Class: pack a personal hygiene bag, pajamas, and slippers for the plane! A little container of baby powder, deodorant, moisturizer, toothbrush and toothpaste, and dry shampoo in your in your carry-on can make a BIG difference in how you feel upon arrival. As for pajamas, wear or pack a comfortable outfit you consider to be "public appropriate." Slippers are great for giving your feet a rest and keep your feet protected when you go to the toilet. The change of clothes and personal supplies will help you relax during your flight and give you a more fresh feeling upon arrival!

In-flight exercise is KEY! Move your legs, ankles, wrists, arms, and hands. GET UP and GET MOVING! Stretch! Run an Internet search for in-flight exercises - and use them!

- Exposure to sunlight helps with correcting the body clock. This can be difficult if you are spending time in an office or meeting room all day. Grabbing a 30 minute walk in daylight can help.

- Avoid naps at the new destination and get on the new sleep schedule as soon as possible. (This may seem impossible, because that nap feels so good! If you can't make it without a nap, limit it to twenty minutes so it doesn't interfere with your night's sleep.)

- Some people use melatonin, an herbal sleep remedy, or a sleep aid to assist sleep on the plane and then those first couple of nights adjusting to a new time zone.

- Some exercise (walking, for example) at the destination can help release tension and bring on sleep.

- Check out the diet tips in *Overcoming Jet Lag* by Dr. Charles Ehret.

A Little Something Extra

An average time for recovering from jet lag is

about one day of recovery for every time zone you have crossed. So when I leave Hong Kong and return to Chicago, my body needs about fourteen days to reset the body clock completely.

There are other useful tips as well when traveling:

- Think about your seat preference when booking your air ticket. If you are by the window you will be stepping over two other people to get to the aisle. If leg room is important, book the flight early and reserve exit row or bulkhead (make sure the seat reclines if you want that).
- Many frequent flyers take vitamin C or Airborne before flying. Some use a triple antibiotic inside their nostrils for flights. Most carry and use hand sanitizer.
- Sitting toward the front of the plane can be an advantage in getting through immigration faster. Plan your restroom visit before deplaning in order to get in the immigration line sooner.
- Stretch and move on the plane, as possible. Invent reasons to get up and walk around. I head

to the back of the plane and stretch, particularly when the flight is longer than eight hours.

- Make sure you are getting what you need in terms of fiber and food when traveling to someplace where food will be very different from what you are used to—and perhaps even different from what you like. I pack flax seed capsules. Other helpful foods to have with you are individual packets of oatmeal and a jar of peanut butter. And getting fresh fruit at your destination to have in the room might be helpful—your body hunger clock may take some adjusting.

- When possible, resist the temptation to be productive on a long flight. You may find you arrive in better shape if you can maximize sleep and maybe read or watch a movie.

- Bring an empty water bottle on the plane with you and fill it there. Buy bottled water when you arrive, keep some in your room, and carry some with you.

- Fill out your immigration and customs forms as soon as you get them and put them with your passport. Keep a pen with you.
- Let your credit card company know you will be out of the country. My card has been canceled before because they thought it had been stolen. Getting this fixed is inconvenient, at best.

Presenting

Congratulations! You made it to your destination! In this chapter, we will discuss the steps you can take to help make the training a success. We will discuss ideas for presenting and facilitating your session. You will want to be prepared for new challenges, and open for change and adapting new techniques.

Choosing the Facilitator

If you are selecting a facilitator who will be successful with global work, these are some characteristics to look for:

- Demonstrates flexibility and adaptability
- Is adventurous
- Demonstrates cultural sensitivity
- Appreciates differences rather than tolerates them

- Builds quick rapport and relationships
- Has solid knowledge of content, is able to focus on participants and learning
- Demonstrates sensitivity to adjustments needed with participants and surroundings
- Awareness of when things aren't working and willingness to improvise for solutions

Working with a Classroom Interpreter

- Help your interpreter to be familiar with your topic and any unfamiliar terms that may be used in your presentation. They can help you with local references, jargon, and colloquialisms. Be sure to ask!
- Schedule a meeting to discuss the program and audience in advance. Share the presentation with your interpreter ahead of time if possible, so he or she will know the major sections and flow of the presentation. It will also give them time to look up specific terms or words. This can be done in person or virtually, with Skype or a tool like Webex or Adobe Connect.

- Establish a comfortable relationship with the interpreter. You want them to be comfortable asking you questions and getting clarification. Ask them how they like to work. This dialogue will help to establish a comfortable relationship during the presentation.
- Make sure you obtain the correct spelling and pronunciation of the interpreter's name, so you can introduce the person.
- Find out if your interpreter is already familiar with the audience, so he or she can give you some insight into what techniques or gestures might be most effective and what should be avoided.
- Ask the interpreter for help if you don't understand what a participant is saying.
- Plan on frequent breaks—your interpreter will need them. Translating is demanding work.
- Do a run-through with your equipment and the interpreter, if possible. This will give peace of mind and help to prevent last minute issues.

Technology Related

- If you have all your material on a memory stick, bring backup. Some countries experience different viruses or copyright issues, so don't let your memory stick or other electronic material out of your sight. Also, back up your files via email or in the cloud.

- Don't share memory drives. My friends and peers in India tell me they have serious virus issues. If I need to share files with them, I put them on a smaller memory stick, just give it to them, and I don't use it again. It seems like a large precaution, but people bring serious viruses home and bringing some low capacity memory sticks with me seems like a small investment.

- Be extra careful using hotel's computer or their wireless network due to virus or hacking issues.

- Call your phone service provider before you go regarding a global plan. *WhatsApp* allows free texting when you have internet.

> *If you are shipping materials, ship separate packages for paper, products, and media (video, flash drives, etc.) A peer was doing training on equipment in China years ago. She shipped one box containing handouts, marketing material, and handheld printers. The whole box was held up in customs because of the equipment, whereas the paper would have sailed right through. As a result, she had no handouts, materials, or equipment samples to use during the training, because it did not arrive until she was already gone.*

Connect with the Group

- Deliberately and intentionally find ways to connect with participants. Let them teach you something you don't know.
- Introduce yourself, any interpreters, and any management or administrative staff who may be in the room, and then graciously thank the appropriate people for inviting you there.

- Start with a team question or exercise in small groups. Ask participants to introduce themselves as they are reporting their answers to the larger group. It may be less intimidating than starting off first thing speaking.

- Use name tents and name badges in class for your benefit as well as theirs. Practice pronouncing names before class if possible.

- Share something about yourself—a photo from home or of you doing something meaningful or wacky is a nice way to connect. Sharing music or movies is another way to cross cultures, because your learners often know American movies and artists.

- Let the group teach you something, such as eating with chopsticks or a new food or a shopping tip.

> *While training in Hong Kong, I saw a fruit I didn't know. I took a photo of it and asked participants over lunch. It looked exactly like a lemon, but it was over six inches long. Four people were looking on their smart phones to find the name in English of the fruit (turned out to be a pomelo). They told me how to eat it, and I picked one up on the way back to the hotel. They asked me about it the next day. It was a great conversation and connection point.*

- Check in with the participants frequently to allow them to ask questions. This is particularly important if people are attending in a non-native language. For them to answer a question, the person needs to translate it to their native language, think about the question, decide if they want to answer it out loud, translate their answer into your language in their head and then answer it. Whew!
- Allow people to see your personality. Be appropriate, but let them see and experience you. It will help them to be more comfortable.

Over lunch in Hong Kong, I remarked that while I was eating with chopsticks, I wasn't really doing it properly and it took me longer to eat with them than a fork. Wow, the group jumped in and started teaching me proper technique. One participant started me with the right grip. The next coached me on the position I was using to grip the chopstick. Another person worked with me to hold one stick still and move the other. They decided on a follow-up practice plan for me and my final test was to eat peanuts with chopsticks. Oh, the pressure! I carried the chopsticks around during breaks and even in the hotel room, practicing and developing muscle memory. The next day at our graduation/celebration dim sum lunch, I ate peanuts with my chopsticks while everyone around me cheered! It was a great bonding event.

Establish Common Goals for the Program

- Participants will be in class for different reasons. Explain that one of the goals of this program is to build on existing knowledge and continue to increase knowledge and skills throughout the program.

- Pre-determine your purpose, intention, what you want to achieve, and how you will measure success.

- Determine how you will measure the effectiveness of the training. Use a feedback form that includes open-ended questions to help them in communicating whether the program met their needs, and to give them the opportunity to ask any follow up questions. Asking for feedback using emoticons (happy or smiley face) can help avoid confusion.

Create an Environment

- Refer participants to the objectives to be achieved and discuss them.

- Show the agenda for the program and explain when and how long breaks will be scheduled, lunch times, etc. If the training is not in their native language, it is important to regularly show where you are in the agenda. It will provide context and help participants stay on track.
- Facilitate a team-building activity where participants work in small groups to discuss a question that is related to the topic and combine their ideas to come up with a summary to briefly present back to the large group can be helpful. Ask questions such as: What do you want to know about this topic? Why is this topic important to you? What do you already know about the topic? How will this topic be helpful to you?
- Thank everyone for their participation.
- Invite people to stop you to ask questions any time throughout the program—this will enable you to slow down enough for those who are not familiar with the language to catch up.

- Be attentive to pace. Language skills may vary and it may affect your agenda. Be flexible and sensitive to their needs or questions.
- Provide regular summaries. It gives an additional chance at clarification.
- Listen intently. Don't hesitate to ask someone to repeat a question or comment.
- Allow extra time for a person to respond to a question.
- Build periodic question-and-answer periods into the program so that even people from cultures that are less likely to ask questions can be encouraged to participate (some Asian groups, for example). Even if the majority of participants are from such a culture, have learners discuss their questions in small groups and then ask them to submit the questions in writing or through a spokesperson. Alternately, have a list of frequently asked questions as a start to the Q & A.
- Use appropriate pictures and graphs to reinforce concepts.

- Show how activities are linked to the course objectives, and refer back to them often. If you find resistance to activities, explain the purpose for the activity. Ask the group how they learn best and it will generally be a mix of auditory, visual, and hands-on (kinesthetic). Make it very transparent what you are doing and why. And if the group still resists the activity, perhaps they are not ready for that—choose a different way to teach it.

Terrence recently connected with a new group in Dubai. He sent a three minute pre-workshop briefing via video before the session. It was a greeting and "to help you get the most of your professional investment" message. He told them he was looking forward to working with them. As participants arrived, they recognized him. He started building rapport before he even met them. This is a low energy effort and high payback way to build a connection with learners and begin to build the safe classroom environment. You can use products like ScreenR or Screencast-O-Matic.

Tips for Adding Interactivity and Fun

- **Plan it.** The first time you want to try a new activity or method, plan it thoroughly. Practice it. Consider in advance the participants' styles, obstacles, or potholes that might come along.

- **Know your audience.** Choose activities that are a good fit and use variety.

- **Try it once with a test group** before you take it to your target audience. Your test run may be with a peer group or at home with neighborhood kids.

> *Do as much as you can with what is comfortable for them. Present in their native language when possible. They are already thrown into something they are not familiar or comfortable with. Let them use their language and do it their way when you can. Acknowledge their customs.*
> *~ Bill Wiggenhorn*

- **Do a run-through** with a couple of colleagues or people you trust. It is good to practice verbal instructions and even more helpful to practice with colleagues that are non-native to the US. It is good to see whether written instructions support the exercise. Where appropriate, have written as well as verbal instructions.

- **Don't do it to do it.** Don't do an exercise for the purpose of doing an exercise. Have a purpose; have a point. Make the connection so learners know why they are doing it. Better yet, let them explain why they just did it.

- **Let 'em fiddle.** Provide highlighters, Post-it® notes, and tactile things to stimulate the senses—Koosh® balls, stress balls, or something for active bodies to handle. Having these items in a classroom to assist fidgeting participants helps them use some energy and other senses as they connect with content.

- **Allow time to reflect/digest.** Leave time in class for participants to list "ah-ha" moments and link those to something they know. Reflection aids learning transfer.

- **Give rationale.** Let participants know why you are using different methodologies; remove the "curtain" so they can see that different methods help different people. People learn by seeing, hearing, and doing. State, *"we have all different learning styles in the room, so we will teach* *using different methods to respect each person in the group. You may find you don't like some of the methods, but it will likely be helping someone in the room."*

Facilitating Tips

- Open with intent to be sensitive. I would say, "It is my intention to be sensitive to your culture. If I do something that is not helpful or is insulting I am sorry, please tell me so I can learn a little something extra."
- Communicate clear goals, and be transparent about accomplishing goals. Prepare and communicate clear verbal and written instructions.
- Plan for breaks—this is especially important, particularly if your participants are thinking a lot outside of their native language. You may need shorter and more frequent breaks than you usually take.
- If possible, have an ally in the room. Develop rapport with someone who will give you the open and direct feedback you are looking for. Ask

them to let you know if something is not clear, if you need to slow down, or if there is a disconnect that needs to be addressed. They can give you a "sign" or they can ask a question directly or let you know during a break.

- Be sure to review your content and know your audience before you select an approach to use. If you are using a new tool, practice it before you are in front of a group or before you send out instructions. Also, when using new methods or tools, be ready to adjust along the way. If an activity is not going well, intervene by giving hints or reviewing the goals or outcome of the activity.

> *A peer heard before doing negotiating training in Japan that they don't like to interact. The first morning of the workshop he asked a question, but everyone just stared at him. He stopped the training and explained that while he was aware that their culture did not typically have a lot of interaction in training, the workshop was built to be interactive and included skills building. He explained that he couldn't effectively teach them to negotiate unless there was dialogue and activities. He eased into it asking questions that required hand raising, some yes and no questions. By the afternoon they had some pretty healthy dialogue going.*

A Little Something Extra

Assist managers with a follow-up plan for each participant based on what you observed in the classroom. Work with your in-country contact or client to determine what should be changed in future programs or locations. Review any areas of confusion that may have come out in observations or on the feedback forms.

Keys to Success

Have we already talked about everything? No, seems there are a few more ideas. Being prepared for multiple cultures and a new destination can help you to be more productive and effective. The goal of this book is to help you to be more successful.

Practice Your Presentation

- Take enough time to practice your entire presentation.
- If possible, practice with someone who will give you feedback.
- Make sure you have contingencies/backup plans that you can smoothly switch to, if something is not working with this audience.

- You should know the key points that must be covered and objectives that must be achieved for your program to be considered successful.
- Plan for enough timing for translation, clarification, and extra breaks if needed.

Check Materials

- Make sure you have enough hard copies and additional electronic storage device copies of your program that you can carry with you, in case materials that have been previously sent are not where you need them.
- Have a plan for distributing your material to the participants.
- Have extra copies of materials, in case additional people drop in unexpectedly.

A Little Something Extra

Geert Hofstede is a thought leader in the area of culture. His research and findings provides some thought-provoking considerations regarding five dimensions when communicating with people of other cultures: power distance, individualism, masculinity, uncertainty avoidance, and long-term orientation.

- In high power distance countries, people expect and accept inequality among people: Mexico, Arab countries, India, West Africa. Low power distance countries are: Greece, Thailand, East Africa, and Colombia.

- Individualism is the degree to which people of a country have learned to act as individuals rather than as members of cohesive groups: Individualism: United States, Australia, Great Britain, and Canada. Collectivism: Colombia, Indonesia, Thailand, West and East Africa.

- Masculinity is the degree to which "masculine" values such as assertiveness and competition prevail over "feminine" values such as warm personal relationships, service, and solidarity. Masculine countries include Japan, Austria, Italy, Switzerland, Mexico. Feminine countries: Brazil, Canada, India, Argentina.

- Uncertainty avoidance is the degree to which people in a country prefer structured over unstructured situations, from extremely rigid to extremely flexible.

High: Greece, Japan, and France.

Low: Denmark, Great Britain, and India.

- Long-term orientation is perseverance and respect for tradition versus short-term orientation and materialism.

  Long-Term: China, Japan, Brazil, and India.

  Short-Term: Canada, Great Britain, United States, and Australia.

  (Jandt, 2004)

Given this information, how do we apply it?

- If there is a large perceived power distance between you as a presenter or teacher and your students, they may be less likely to ask you the questions that they want to ask you. So you can write some typical questions and answers and provide them in a handout, thus shortening the time allotted for questions and answers during your program.
- If there is a strong sense of cohesiveness among members of a culture, you can provide

opportunities to discuss topics in small groups, in addition to offering opportunities to answer questions individually.

- A strong "masculine" culture may respond well to competitive learning games, whereas a strong "feminine" culture may respond better to group events that provide time to get to know each other.

- Uncertainty avoidance cultures will be more successful if the program is highly structured. Provide some flexibility during small group conversations and breaks that can satisfy the needs of participants who look for these opportunities.

- Long-term orientation cultures will expect to know the effects over time of learning the information that is being presented, whereas, the short-term orientated culture requires that you explain immediate payback for the time and money invested in the program.

I love the proposition of considering Brazil as one of the "feminine countries." I would really like to reinforce this fact. One day, I was starting a sales workshop for a group of 12 directors who worked for the same company. Half of the audience had a Brazilian nationality while the other 50% came from different countries (mainly from Europe and Asia). I realized that the narrative of the Brazilians was very powerful for engaging the other person in sales dialogue. That generated a big discussion in the group, as we proceeded with feedback on the exercise. Not all the Europeans accepted the "feminine" approach of the Brazilians. But at the end they had to recognize the Brazilians were very good at using their communication style to provide emotional reasons for doing business. This generated a positive impact on doing business and getting the "yes" from their customers.
~ Alfredo Castro

Some Other Keys to Success

- Listen carefully to understand questions and comments, especially if someone's accent is difficult to understand. Don't be afraid to ask people to repeat. You can say, "*Will you repeat and speak slower? I am getting accustomed to your accent.*" And don't forget: to them YOU have an accent.

- Make reference to your agenda and objectives periodically, so participants always know where you are in your program. Summarize each topic and explain what you will be covering next.

- Ensure that your visuals are tasteful for the cultures that may be represented by participants in your program. Have someone review the program ahead of time and provide feedback to you to assure there are no potential insults, mistakes, or confusion.

> As a rule, I find we are almost always our harshest critics. Remember there is no end game, only process. Have realistic expectations of yourself.
> ~Charles Gremillion

A colleague learned not to make assumptions. She was presenting on a topic in Japan. She was the only female in the room, as she talked she noticed people not looking at her and not making eye contact. They were looking inattentive, no one answered her questions. She switched to a lecture, which was not her plan. Later in discussions, they knew everything she presented. In some instances they recited word for word. She had made an assumption that they didn't care or weren't paying attention. Be careful about making assumptions.

A Little Something Extra

In addition to time, language and personal space differences, misunderstandings can occur among cultures in areas such as roles, status, values, the importance of the group or individual, and approach to work. It is important for each of us to not assume that we know what is going on in cross-cultural communications, but to test our assumptions and be open to other possible interpretations of people's behavior and language.

There is Always Something Extra to Learn

Many people are eager to experience global opportunities so they can taste the food, explore the geography, and learn about cultures. But traveling to global destinations and presenting to diverse groups of people can be challenging if you are not prepared. Hopefully, you have picked up tips and ideas here. Researching before you go and being attentive while you are there will help you understand different cultures and people better. It may even get rid of some of the distractions that can get in the way of learning transfer.

One thing I have learned from studying from some amazingly talented people is, there is not a "there" when learning about other cultures. You don't learn everything about cultures; you learn an awareness and sensitivity. You learn about their customs to be respectful. You learn to scan for things and then to be open to reacting as needed. Just as American audiences vary, audiences in other countries will vary. They will be different based on their education, upbringing, learning preferences, professions, and more.

I think you will find there is always something extra to learn. I work in the workplace learning and performance field. Folks in my tribe thrive in the world of gaining knowledge and skills. What a great opportunity to develop and grow ourselves—and continue to see the world differently.

Contributors

Information from this book has come from many places—experience over the years, watching and listening to peers. Thanks to some of the folks that have directly provided information or editing assistance:

Alfredo Castro

Leonard Cochran

Vince Cyboran

Terrence Donahue

Kit Libenschek

Charles Gremillion

Kimberly Seeger

Vikas Sheth

Sandy Stricker

Trish Uhl

Bill Wiggenhorn

Source

Hofstede, G. (2004). Business Cultures. *UNESCO Courier, 1994.* In F. Jandt (Ed.), *Intercultural Communication: A Global Reader.* Thousand Oaks, CA: Sage.

Jandt, F. (2004). *An Introduction to Intercultural Communication: Identities in a Global Community.* Thousand Oaks, CA: Sage.

About Learniappe

Learn a Little Something Extra!

Learniappe is a solutions-focused advisory and support firm with extensive experience and enigmatic passion for continued learning. Learniappe was inspired by the French term, Lagniappe, which means to give more or an extra benefit.

Learniappe occurs when we learn something extra and add to our knowledge, skills and experiences.

Extra Books by Learniappe:

111 Questions to Design Learning

111 Quotes to Inspire Learning

111 Creative Ways to Use QR Codes in Learning

111 Apps for the Learning Professional's Toolkit

111 Ideas for an Influential Presentation

Books are available on Amazon.

LEARN *iappe*

About the Author

Renie McClay is a global learning consultant who is passionate about connecting with people—from many cultures, on many topics, and on many levels.

Renie has managed the training function for several Fortune 500 companies, including Kraft, Novartis, and Pactiv (makers of Hefty). After 20 years in corporate training and development roles, she started her own firm, Inspired Learning LLC.

Possessing a passion for travel, Renie has been to over 38 countries and enjoys getting to know new cultures. Her audiences have included people across the globe from Australia, Europe, Asia, Middle East, Latin America, and North America. She facilitates in a classroom and virtually.

Renie is Adjunct Faculty for Roosevelt University and Concordia University. She also consults on a wide variety of sales and learning initiatives and is a facilitator for American Management Association. She designs and delivers training for increased performance. She is a Certified Professional of Learning and Performance (CPLP) and has a Masters in Global Talent Development from DePaul University. She is an honoree of the International Business Award and the Stevie Award for Women.

Connect!

Inspiring Clarity Blog: www.inspiredtolearn.net/blog

Twitter: http://twitter.com/reniemcclay

LinkedIn: www.linkedin.com/in/reniemcclay

Website: www.inspiredtolearn.net

Email: info@inspiredtolearn.net

Other Books by Renie McClay:

10 Steps to Successful Teams (ASTD Press)

The Essential Guide to Training Global Audiences (Pfeiffer)

Fortify Your Sales Force: Leading and Training Exceptional Teams (Pfeiffer)

Interactive and Engaging Training (Inspired Learning LLC)

More Praise!

I have had the privilege of working with Renie on some specific global projects - and I admire her knowledge! Even after learning and sharing with her experiences about global audiences I have had a very useful learning experience after reading this book! She shares ideas to engage audiences from all over the world.

-Alfredo Castro, *President, MOT Training and Development, Brazil*

I have known Renie and watched her travels to places like India, China, Europe, Hong Kong and the Middle East. I love hearing the stories of the cultures and the interactions. How great to see the tips from those experiences shared! Better to learn from other's experiences than from the international school of hard knocks!

-Jann Iaco, *CPLP, eLearning and Training Specialist, Global Home Furnishings Retailer*

Renie McClay's book, *111 Ideas for Engaging Global Audiences*, is a must-have for any business professional traveling outside the country, especially first-timers. Pulling from her years of experience and countless trips abroad, Renie gives insight on how to be successful in a global setting. It is practical and easy to implement.

-Sarah Jeffcoat, *Learning and Performance Consultant, CEFCU*

In this installment of the Learniappe 111 series of books, Renie has delivered a powerful tool that should be read by anyone who travels abroad for training. Don't travel alone; taking this book with you is like having a seasoned professional with you the whole time.

-Larry Straining, *CPLP, Larry's Training, LLC*

Renie McClay has done it again and knocked this one out of the ballpark! What a great resource for anyone who finds themselves traveling abroad. This book will certainly be on my packing list of must-haves the next time I find myself traveling around the globe!

-Debbie Myrand, *Vice President of Membership, Mid Michigan ASTD*

57

18790346R00035

Made in the USA
Charleston, SC
20 April 2013